Sport Balls Crochet

Great Toys for Sport-enthusiast Kids

DEDICATION

Contents

Soccer Ball

Materials

1 skein each of black and white worsted weight yarn (I really like how cotton holds up for this)

US G-6 / 4.0 mm crochet hook

fiberfill stuffing

scissors and yarn needle

Finished crochet soccer ball measures approx. 16½ in. around

PENTAGON (MAKE 12)

With black yarn, make a magic ring (as an alternative to the magic ring, you can ch 4 and join with a slip stitch in furthest chain from hook to form a ring).

Round 1: Work 10 sc in the ring, join with a Sl st in first sc made — 10 sts.

Round 2: Without turning your work, ch 2 (counts as hdc), 1 hdc in next st, ch 2, *1 hdc in each of the next 2 sts, ch 2, repeat from * 3 more times, join to top of ch-2 from beginning of round — 20 sts.

Fasten off and weave in ends.

HEXAGON (MAKE 20)

With white yarn, make magic ring or use alternate method described above.

Round 1: Work 12 sc in ring, join with a Sl st in first sc made, pull tail of yarn to close up ring — 12 sts.

Round 2: Without turning your work, ch 2 (counts as hdc), 1 hdc in next st, ch 2, * 1 hdc in each of the next 2 sts, ch 2, repeat from * 4 more times, join to top of ch-2 from beginning of round — 24 sts.

Fasten off and weave in ends.

FINISHING

Now we are going to turn all those crochet pieces into a soccer ball! Using the illustration above as a guide to placement, Sl st pieces together through back loops only and with right sides facing.

When only one piece remains, stuff ball with polyester fiberfill to desired consistency. Use a tapestry needle to whip stitch remaining piece in place.

Football

Supplies

Brown worsted weight yarn (I used Red Heart Super Saver)

5.0 mm crochet hook

Yarn Needle

Scissors

Polyfil

Non-toxic puffy paint OR white worsted weight yarn

Finished Size: Approximately 7"

Pattern Notes

This pattern is worked in continuous rounds. I recommend using a stitch marker to keep track of the first stitch of the round.

I embellished my football with non-toxic puffy paint. You could also use white yarn if you prefer!

I started stuffing my football after Round 28. I gradually added more stuffing until the I reached the end. I stuffed mine so that it is packed tight!

Instructions

ch 2

Round 1: In the 2nd chain from the hook, SC four times (4)

Round 2: 2 SC in each stitch around (8)

Round 3: *2 SC, SC in next st, repeat from * around (12)

Round 4: SC around (12)

Round 5: *2 SC, SC in next 2 sts, repeat from * around (16)

Round 6: SC around (16)

Round 7: *2 SC, SC in next 3 sts, repeat from * around (20)

Round 8: SC around (20)

Round 9: *2 SC, SC in next 4 sts, repeat from * around (24)

Round 10: SC around (24)

Round 11: *2 SC, SC in next 5 sts, repeat from * around (28)

Round 12: SC around (28)

Round 13: *2 SC, SC in next 6, repeat from * around (32)

Round 14: *2 SC, SC in next 7, repeat from * around (36)

Round 15: *2 SC, SC in next 8, repeat from * around (40)

Round 16-20: SC around (40)

Round 21: *SC2Tog, SC in next 8, repeat from * around (36)

Round 22: *SC2Tog, SC in next 7, repeat from * around (32)

Round 23: *SC2Tog, SC in next 6, repeat from * around (28)

Round 24: SC around (28)

Round 25: *SC2Tog, SC in next 5, repeat from * around (24)

Round 26: SC around (24)

Round 27: *SC2Tog, SC in next 4, repeat from * around (20)

Round 28: SC around (20)

Round 29: *SC2Tog, SC in next 3, repeat from * around (16)

Round 30: SC around (16)

Round 31: *SC2Tog, SC in next 2, repeat from * around (12)

Round 32: SC around (12)

Round 33: *SC2Tog, SC in next st, repeat from * around (8)

Round 34: *SC2Tog, repeat from * around (4)

Tie off leaving a long tail. Use a yarn needle to sew the end shut and weave in ends. Add embellishment with white puffy paint.

Touch Down! You're done!

Baseball

Difficulty: Beginner

Materials

- Crochet Hook, Size E/3.5 mm hook
- Stitch Marker(s)
- Scissors
- Stuffing
- Tapestry Needle
- Chopstick, dowel, or something similar to help with stuffing

- Yarnspirations Caron One Pound (worsted 4-Medium, 100% acrylic, Approx. 812 yds/742 m, 16 oz/453.6 g), Color (A) White, 1 skein, Color (B) Scarlet, a small amount

Design Notes

This pattern is written using US crochet terminology. I chose to use a size E crochet hook. That said, the ultimate desired result is to achieve a tight crochet fabric that when stuffed will not allow the stuffing show through. If a different sized hook works better for you, then by all means, use it! Do note, however, that if you change the hook size or the type of yarn you are using, that this will have an effect on the size and look of your finished item.

This pattern is written primarily in rows.

At the end of each row, I will note in parenthesis how many stitches you should have once completed.

Exact gauge is not essential to this project, but tension should be maintained.

One skein of the yarn used will make a lot of baseballs!

Abbreviations/Stitches Used

ch – Chain

Sport Balls Crochet

Rows – Rows

sc – Single crochet

sc2tog – Single crochet 2 stitches together (decrease)

sl st – Slip stitch

st(s) – Stitch(s)

[ ] – Work instructions between brackets as many times as directed

Finished Measurements

About 12 inches/ 30.48 cm in circumference.

Baseball Pieces

Make 2

Using Color (A)

Chain 4

Row 1: 2sc in the 2nd chain from the hook, sc, 2sc in the last st (5sts)

Row 2: Ch 1, turn, 2sc in the 1st st, [sc] 3 times, 2sc in the last st (7sts)

Row 3: Ch 1, turn, 2sc in the 1st st, [sc] 5 times, 2sc in the last st (9sts)

Row 4: Ch 1, turn, 2sc in the 1st st, [sc] 7 times, 2sc in the last st (11sts)

Sport Balls Crochet

Row 5: Ch 1, turn, 2sc in the 1st st, [sc] 9 times, 2sc in the last st (13sts)

Row 6: Ch 1, turn, sc in each st across (13sts)

Row 7: Ch 1, turn, sc2tog, [sc] 9 times, sc2tog (11sts)

Row 8: Ch 1, turn, sc2tog, [sc] 7 times, sc2tog (9sts)

Rows 9-15: Ch1, turn, sc in each st across (9sts for 7 rows)

Row 16: Ch 1, turn, sc2tog, [sc] 5 times, sc2tog (7sts)

Rows 17-19: Ch1, turn, sc in each st across (7sts for 3 rows)

Row 20: Ch 1, turn, sc2tog, [sc] 3 times, sc2tog (5sts)

Row 21: Ch1, turn, sc in each st across (5sts)

Row 22: Ch 1, turn, 2sc in the 1st st, [sc] 3 times, 2sc in the last st (7sts)

Rows 23-25: Ch1, turn, sc in each st across (7sts for 3 rows)

Row 26: Ch 1, turn, 2sc in the 1st st, [sc] 5 times, 2sc in the last st (9sts)

Rows 27-33: Ch1, turn, sc in each st across (9sts for 7 rows)

Row 34: Ch 1, turn, 2sc in the 1st st, [sc] 7 times, 2sc in the last st (11sts)

Row 35: Ch 1, turn, 2sc in the 1st st, [sc] 9 times, 2sc in the last st (13sts)

Row 36: Ch1, turn, sc in each st across (13sts)

Row 37: Ch 1, turn, sc2tog, [sc] 9 times, sc2tog (11sts)

Row 38: Ch 1, turn, sc2tog, [sc] 7 times, sc2tog (9sts)

Row 39: Ch 1, turn, sc2tog, [sc] 5 times, sc2tog (7sts)

Row 40: Ch 1, turn, sc2tog, [sc] 3 times, sc2tog (5sts)

Row 41: Ch 1, turn, sc2tog, sc, sc2tog (3sts)

You're now going to smooth out the outer edge of your piece and create the stitches that you will use to stitch your ball together. Ch 1, sc in the same space. Now evenly sc around the entire outer edge of the piece, putting two sc in the same space when rounding corners. You'll want to do this as consistently as you can on both pieces so that you have the same number of stitches to work into when you're stitching your ball together with the red yarn. You can fudge it a little if needed so don't over stress it, but it will be helpful to try to create a similar number of stitches on both pieces.

Once you have sc around the entire edge sl st to the 1st st and fasten off. Weave in your ends.

Stitching Your Pieces Together

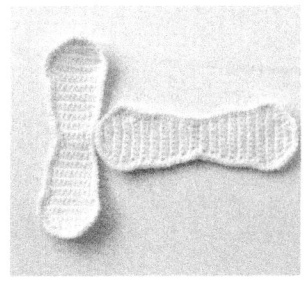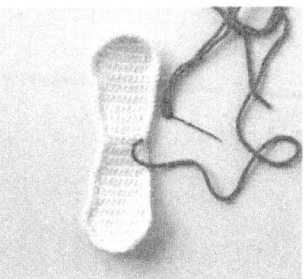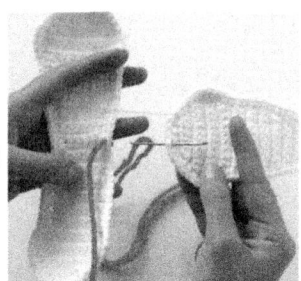

Using Color (B)

This part is not too complicated but there are a couple things that you'll want to pay attention to, to make sure that your pieces line up as they should. I found it most helpful to find the center stitch on both pieces on at the top center and on at the middle center. These are the first two stitches that you will work into. If it's helpful, you can fold your pieces in half accordingly to help determine which stitches you want. You'll be working in those single crochet stitches you made while crocheting around the outer edge of your pieces.

The baseball stitch is done by coming up through the bottom of your work to the top every time and alternating back and forth between piece one and piece two. Because I tried to make sure that I had the same number of stitches on both pieces when I crocheted around the edge earlier I was able to just catch every stitch and it lined up amazingly. Ultimately, the goal is for the top center and the middle center to line up at every turn as you are stitching. If it's helpful you

13

can pin these points together or pull them together using a stitch marker. You can fudge things a little by skipping a stitch now and then if needed to keep the center points lined up, but your stitching will look most professional if you take the time to go through as many stitches as possible between these points.

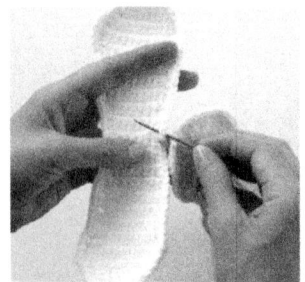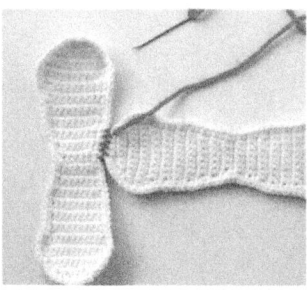

When you get towards the end of stitching your ball is likely to look a bit misshapen. Just make sure that you have your centers lined up and then firmly stuff and shape your piece. It will round out and look like the baseball you are wanting. When you finish with your final stitch just draw one last stitch through both piece, knot off, and weave in your end.

>Design Tip: Add stuffing right up to the very end of stitching your piece closed. Use a chopstick or other similar item as the hole gets smaller. You don't want to overstuff to where you're pulling your stitches apart making the stuffing show, but firmly packed and shaped will create a more professional looking piece.

Basketball

MATERIALS:

2mm crochet hook,

orange and black yarn dk yarn,

stuffing material,

sewing needle,

scissors.

The finished size must be around 10cm.

BALL

With orange color yarn start,

1 row: 6sc in a magic ring

2 row: 6inc Total 12sts

3 row: (1sc, 1inc) repeat 6 times Total 18sts

4 row: 2sc, 1inc) repeat 6 times Total 24sts

5 row: (3sc, 1inc) repeat 6 times Total 30sts

6 row: (4sc, 1inc) repeat 6 times Total 36sts

7 row: (5sc, 1inc) repeat 6 times Total 42sts

8 row: (6sc, 1inc) repeat 6 times Total 48sts

9 row: (7sc, 1inc) repeat 6 times Total 54sts

10 row: (8sc, 1inc) repeat 6 times Total 60sts

11 to 19 row: 60sc

20 row: (8sc, 1dec) repeat 6 times Total 54sts

21 row: (7sc, 1dec) repeat 6 times Total 48sts

22 row: (6sc, 1dec) repeat 6 times Total 42sts

23 row: (5sc, 1dec) repeat 6 times Total 36sts

24 row: (4sc, 1dec) repeat 6 times Total 30sts

25 row: (3sc, 1dec) repeat 6 times Total 24sts

26 row: (2sc, 1dec) repeat 6 times Total 18sts

Stop here for stuffing the ball!

27 row: (1sc, 1dec) repeat 6 times Total 12sts

Cut the yarn, fasten it off, and hid the remaining tail inside the ball.

ASSEMBLY

With black yarn, make a single line in the middle of the ball, horizontal and vertical. This will give you a starting point to make the sidelines.

Sew two other black lines in the central part (see picture).

Volleyball

Materials

I used a size J hook. I didn't pay to much attention to gauge. If you are wanting to get the exact size of an official volleyball, then you might want to use a size or two smaller hook.

White, navy, and grey yarn.

Crochet Volleyball pattern

Crochet hook size J

With white, chain 27

Double crochet in 3rd chain from hook, and continue to double crochet in each stitch across.

Row 2: Chain 2, turn, double crochet in each stitch across

Row 3: Chain 2, turn, double crochet in each stitch across

Break yarn and finish off.

Turn strip upside down and slip stitch in bottom beginning chain. Single crochet in each stitch across and break yarn and finish off.

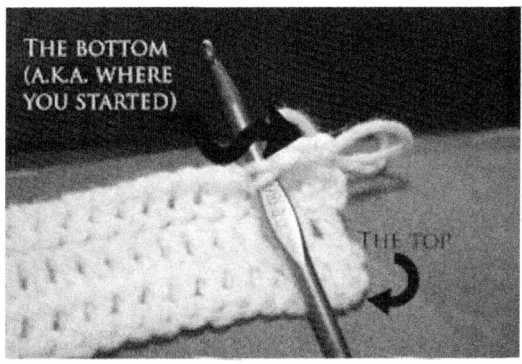

With Gray, slip stitch to join (on either end of the white strip)

Chain 2, double crochet in each stitch across.

Row 2: chain 2, turn, double crochet 2 together, double crochet across the row until you have 2 spaces left, double crochet2 together.

Break off yarn (be sure to leave a long tail of yarn to stitch with)

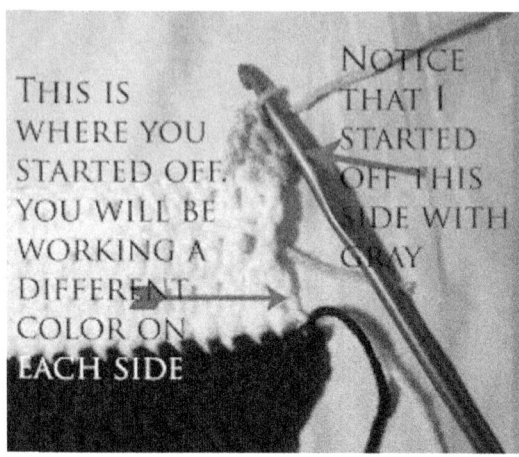

Row 3: repeat row 2

With Navy, repeat what you did with the Gray, only on the other side of the white strip.

Make 6 of these sections and then sew them together with a yarn needle.

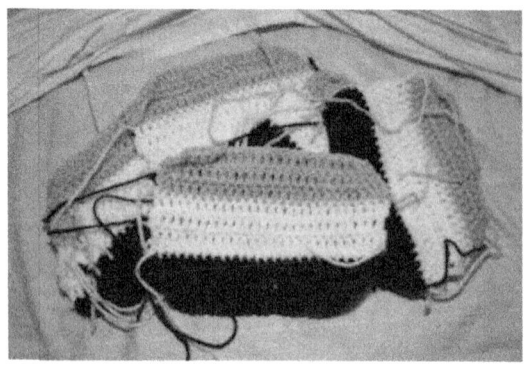

Make sure you sew them facing opposite directions like a real volleyball

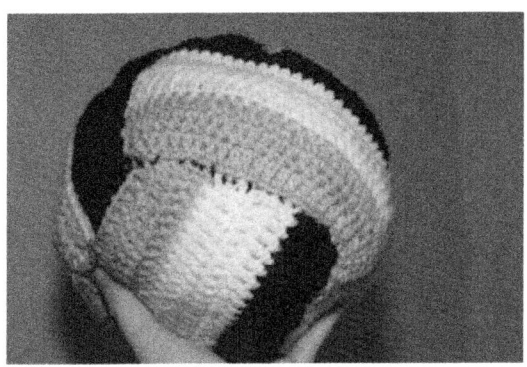

I stuffed the ball with some fiberfill before I sewed up the last section. I was afraid that the fiberfill might poke through between the crochets, so I put some quilt batting around the inside (so of lining the ball). It ended up being a nice soft squishy ball. If you want a harder more bouncyish ball, you might try sewing your sections over a cheap kids rubber ball. the only downside to that would be that if your ball looses air or pops, then you are going to have to take the whole thing apart to replace it.

Tennis Ball

Skill level: Intermediate

Materials:

- Two colors amigurumi yarn with suitable crochet hook

- Needle

- Stuffing

Abbreviations

MR – Magic ring

st – stitch

sl st – slip stitch

Sport Balls Crochet

ch – chain

sc – single crochet

hdc – half double crochet

dc – double crochet

sc2tog – 2 single crochet together

BL – back loop only

FL – front loop only

Special terms:

Invisible slip stitch/Invisible join

Directions:

Tennis ball contain two parts using the following pattern.

You need
two pieces
to crochet one
tennis ball

Rnd 1: MR, ch 2 (does not count as st), 12 dc in the ring, sl st in first dc. (12 dc)

Rnd 2: Ch 2 (does not count as st), 2 dc in each st around, sl st in first dc or use the invisible sl st. FO and weave in ends. (24 dc)

Make a second circle using the same pattern above, make sure to use normal sl st at the end of it and DO NOT FO. Next steps will be in rows.

R 1: Ch 1, turn, hdc, sc in each of next 4 sts, hdc. (6 sts)

R 2: Ch 1, turn, sc in each of next 2 sts, sc2tog, sc in each of next 2 sts. (5 sc)

R 3: Ch 1, turn, sc in each st. (5 sc)

R 4: Ch 1, turn, sc in each st. (5 sc)

R 5: Ch 1, turn, sc in each of next 2 sts, 2 sc, sc in each of next 2 sts. (6 sc)

R 6: Ch 1, turn, hdc, sc in each of next 4 sts, hdc last. Do not FO.

We'll be joining the working piece with the first circle.

Crochet through
both loops of
each piece

6 slip stitches
to join

Wrong sides up

Holding the working piece, ch 1, turn, make sure the first circle is on the wrong side.

Join the two pieces together using sl st through two loops of each side (6 sl st total)

FO and weave in ends.

FO at the end

Repeat same steps from the beginning to make the second piece of the tennis ball. (See pics)

Joining:

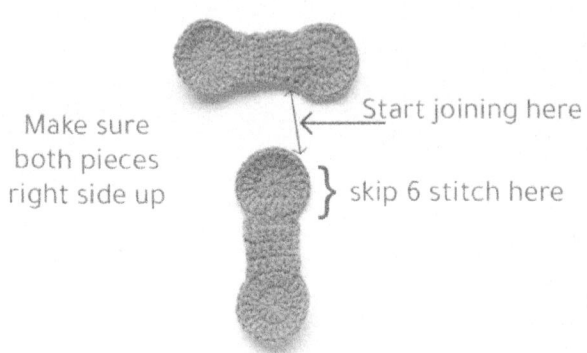

Make sure both pieces right side up

Start joining here

} skip 6 stitch here

Make sure the two piece are right side up.

Using different color, slip knot on the hook, skip next 6 sts after the end of the straight edge, insert the hook BL of next st.

Insert the hook in the first st of the straight edge of the second piece (use one loop only).

Start joining using slip stitches along the edges, make sure to use the BL of the first piece sts and the FL of the second piece (the inner loops

Note that the straight edge equals 6 sts, and the round edge 18 sts.

Start stuffing before you finish the joining. Invisible sl st at the end. FO and weave in ends. Your tennis ball is done!

Beach Ball

Difficulty: Easy

MATERIALS

Acrylic yarn in a variation of 7 Colors including a white color (DK Light)

Polyester fiberfill

Jingle bell (optional)

TOOLS

2.5mm hook

Scissors

INSTRUCTIONS

1. Prepare 7 yarn colors, preferably 1 white and 6 vibrant colors to give a happy summer feel.
2. Crochet the ball by following the crochet pattern stated below.
3. Stuff the ball as instructed
4. Continue to crochet and close the opening of the beach ball.

Abbreviations

sc: single crochet

inc: 2sc increase

inv dec: invisible decrease

sl knot: slip knot

slst: slip stitch

AMIGURUMI PATTERN

Begin with white yarn:

Round 1: sc 6 in magic ring {6}

Round 2: [inc] 6 times. {12}

Round 3: [inc, sc] 6 times. {18}

slst to the back loop of next st (don't count as a stitch).

Fasten.

Change yarn colors (6 colors in a round)

Round 4: make a sl knot on the hook and insert the hook in the first stitch of the round, *[sc 2, inc] repeat each set *[] with new yarn color, a total of 6 sets. {24}

Round 5: *[sc, inc, sc 2] repeat each set *[] by following the color of the previous round, a total of 6 sets. {30}

Round 6: *[sc 4, inc] repeat each set *[] by following the color of the previous round, a total of 6 sets. {36}

Round 7: *[sc 2, inc, sc 3] repeat each set by following the color of the previous round, a total of 6 sets. {42}

Round 8: *[sc 6, inc] repeat each set *[] by following the color of the previous round, a total of 6 sets. {48}

Round 9-16: *[sc 8] repeat each set *[] by following the color of the previous round, a total of 6 sets. {48}

Round 17: *[inv dec, sc 6] repeat each set *[] by following the color of the previous round, a total of 6 sets. {42}

Round 18: *[sc 3, inv dec, sc 2] repeat each set *[] by following the color of the previous round, a total of 6 sets. {36}

Round 19: *[inv dec, sc 4] repeat each set *[] by following the color of the previous round, a total of 6 sets. {30}

Round 20: *[sc 2, inv dec, sc] repeat each set *[] by following the color of the previous round, a total of 6 sets. {24}

Round 21: *[inv dec, sc 2] repeat each set *[] by following the color of the previous round, a total of 6 sets. {18}

slst to the back loop of next st (don't count as a stitch).

Fasten.

Stuff with polyester fillings.

Change yarn to white color

Round 22: make a sl knot on the hook and insert the hook in the first stitch of the round, [sc, inv dec] 6 times. {12}

Round 23: [inv dec] 6 times. {6}

Fasten and sew to close the opening. Hide yarn.

NOTES

Depending on the speed and hours you are spending on the project, the total time needed is only an approximation.

Stuff the ball firmly and densely to give a good shape to the amigurumi.

Bowling Pins & Ball

Materials

worsted-weight yarn in white (approx. 300-450 yd.), red (approx. 156 yd), gray (approx. 156 yd) , and a small amount of black (shown here in Lion Brand Vanna's Choice in White – 100, Scarlet – 113, and Charcoal Grey – 151)

US H-8 / 5 mm crochet hook or smaller depending on your tension (see notes) yarn needle

stitch markers (optional)

fiberfill stuffing

bean bags (optional; see notes)

Notes:

Please note that as with all crochet toys and baby items, this crochet bowling set should be checked regularly for pulls or unraveling stitches that may allow stuffing to come out and become a choking hazard. As always, infants and small children should be supervised.

Use whatever hook size allows you to achieve a nice tight fabric. The tighter the gauge the better the shape and structure of each piece will be.

Use bean bags in the base of each pin and in the center of the ball to add a little weight. To make your own, use uncooked rice or dried beans and place between two squares of fabric. Sew closed at each side, making sure the contents cannot come out. Filling an old sock (with no holes, of course) works great too!

Finished crochet bowling pins measure approximately 9½ in. high x 10 in. around. Finished crochet bowling ball measures approximately

18 in. around.

BOWLING PIN PATTERN

Make 6 pins for a fun kid set or 10 for a standard bowling set.

With white, make a magic ring (as an alternative to the magic ring, you can ch 4 and join with a slip stitch in furthest chain from hook to form a ring).

Round 1: Ch 1 (does not count as st here and throughout), work 6 sc into ring, join - 6 sts.

Round 2: Ch 1, 2 sc in each st around, join - 12 sts.

Round 3: Ch 1, 1 sc in same st as join and each st around, join - 12 sts.

Round 4: Ch 1, beginning is same st as join,*work 2 sc, 1 sc in next, rep from * around, join - 18 sts.

Round 5: Ch 1, 1 sc in same st as join and each st around, join - 18 sts.

Round 6: Ch 1, beginning is same st as join,*work 2 sc, 1 sc in each of the next 2 sts, rep from * around, join - 24 sts.

Rounds 7 through 10: Ch 1, 1 sc in same st as join and each st around, join - 24 sts.

Round 11: Ch 1, beginning is same st as join,*sc2tog, 1 sc in each of the next 2 sts, rep from * around, join and drop white yarn - 18 sts.

Round 12: Join red yarn, ch 1, 1 sc in same st as join and each st around, join - 18 sts.

Round 13: Ch 1, beginning is same st as join,*sc2tog, 1 sc in next st, rep from * around, join and drop red yarn - 12 sts.

Rounds 14 and 15: Pick up and join white yarn, ch 1, 1 sc in same st as join and each st around, join and drop white yarn - 12 sts.

Round 16: Pick up and join red yarn, ch 1, 1 sc in same st as join and each st around, join - 12 sts.

Round 17: Ch 1, beginning is same st as join,*work 2 sc, 1 sc in next, rep from * around, join and fasten off red yarn - 18 sts.

Round 18: Pick up and join white, ch 1, 1 sc in same st as join and each st around, join - 18 sts.

Round 19: Ch 1, beginning is same st as join,*work 2 sc, 1 sc in each of the next 2 sts, rep from * around, join - 24 sts.

Stuff tip of pin at this point, taking care not to over stuff.

Round 20: Ch 1, 1 sc in same st as join and each st around, join - 24 sts.

Round 21: Ch 1, beginning is same st as join,*work 2 sc, 1 sc in each of the next 3 sts, rep from * around, join - 30 sts.

Rounds 22 through 31: Ch 1, 1 sc in same st as join and each st around, join - 30 sts.

Round 32: Ch 1, beginning is same st as join,*sc2tog, 1 sc in each of the next 3 sts, rep from * around, join - 24 sts.

Rounds 33 through 35: Ch 1, 1 sc in same st as join and each st around, join - 24 sts.

Round 36: Ch 1, 1 sc in same st as join and each st around, join - 24 sts.

Round 37: Ch 1, beginning is same st as join and working in back loops only for this round, *sc2tog, 1 sc in each of the next 2 sts, rep from * around, join - 18 sts.

Stuff rest of pin at this point, taking care not to over stuff. If using a bean bag, place in last so it is at base of pin (see notes).

Round 38: Ch 1, beginning is same st as join and work *sc2tog, 1 sc in next st, rep from * around, join - 12 sts.

Round 39: Ch 1, beginning is same st as join,sc2tog around, join - 6 sts.

Fasten off and leave a tail of about 6 inches long. Using a tapestry needle, weave the tail through each stitch and pull gently to tighten. Weave in ends.

CROCHET BOWLING BOWL PATTERN

With gray yarn, make a magic ring.

Round 1: Ch 1, work 6 sc into ring, join - 6 sts.

Round 2: Ch 1, 2 sc in each st around, join - 12 sts.

Round 3: Ch 1, beginning is same st as join,*work 2 sc, 1 sc in next, rep from * around, join - 18 sts.

Round 4: Ch 1, beginning is same st as join,*work 2 sc, 1 sc in each of the next 2 sts, rep from * around, join - 24 sts.

Round 5: Ch 1, beginning is same st as join,*work 2 sc, 1 sc in each of the next 3 sts, rep from * around, join - 30 sts.

Round 6: Ch 1,beginning is same st as join,*work 2 sc, 1 sc in each of the next 4 sts, rep from * around, join - 36 sts.

Round 7: Ch 1, beginning is same st as join,*work 2 sc, 1 sc in each of the next 5 sts, rep from * around, join - 42 sts.

Round 8: Ch 1, beginning is same st as join,*work 2 sc, 1 sc in each of the next 6 sts, rep from * around, join - 48 sts.

Round 9: Ch 1, beginning is same st as join,*work 2 sc, 1 sc in each of the next 7 sts, rep from * around, join - 54 sts.

Round 10: Ch 1, beginning is same st as join,*work 2 sc, 1 sc in each of the next 8 sts, rep from * around, join - 60 sts.

Rounds 11 through 20: Ch 1, 1 sc in same st as join and each st around, join - 60 sts.

Round 21: Ch 1, beginning is same st as join and work *sc2tog, 1 sc in each of the next 8 sts, rep from * around, join - 54 sts.

Round 22: Ch 1, beginning is same st as join and work *sc2tog, 1 sc in each of the next 7 sts, rep from * around, join - 48 sts.

Round 23: Ch 1, beginning is same st as join and work *sc2tog, 1 sc in each of the next 6 sts, rep from * around, join - 42 sts.

Round 24: Ch 1, beginning is same st as join and work *sc2tog, 1 sc in each of the next 5 sts, rep from * around, join - 36 sts.

Round 25: Ch 1, beginning is same st as join and work *sc2tog, 1 sc in each of the next 4 sts, rep from * around, join - 30 sts.

Round 26: Ch 1, beginning is same st as join and work *sc2tog, 1 sc in each of the next 3 sts, rep from * around, join - 24 sts.

Stuff ball, taking care not to over stuff. If using a bean bag, position it in the center of the ball.

Round 27: Ch 1, beginning is same st as join and work *sc2tog, 1 sc in each of the next 2 sts, rep from * around, join - 18 sts.

Round 28: Ch 1, beginning is same st as join and work *sc2tog, 1 sc in next st, rep from * around, join - 12 sts.

Round 29: Ch 1, beginning is same st as join, sc2tog around, join - 6 sts.

Fasten off and leave a tail of about 6 inches long. Using a tapestry needle, weave the tail through each stitch and pull gently to tighten. Weave in ends.

Faux Finger Holes (make 3)

With black yarn, make a magic ring.

Round 1: Ch 1, work 6 sc into ring, join - 6 sts.

For best results, use the invisible join and fasten off method. Leave a tail of about 6 inches long. Using a yarn needle, sew faux finger holes to ball as shown in pictures. Weave in ends.

Sport Balls Baby Blanket and Rattles

SKILL LEVEL: INTERMEDIATE

Materials

RED HEART® Super Saver®: 5 skeins 847 Blue Tones A, 1 skein

each 336 Warm Brown B, 316 Soft White C, 256 Carrot D, 312 Black E, and 376 Burgundy F

Susan Bates® Crochet Hooks: 3.75mm [F-5 US] (for rattle seam lines), 4mm [G-6 US] (for rattles), 5mm [H-8 US] (for appliques), and 5.5mm [I-9 US] (for blanket)

Yarn needle, large embroidery needle, stitch marker, small amount of stuffing, cat toy for each rattle insert, knee high for each rattle insert, black sewing thread and sewing needle

GAUGE: 11 sts = 4" (10 cm) in half double crochet; 8½ rows = 4" (10 cm) with largest hook. CHECK YOUR GAUGE. Use any size hook to obtain the gauge.

Blanket measures 36" x 36" (91.5 x 91.5 cm).

ABBREVIATIONS

A, B, C = Color A, Color B, Color C, etc.;

sp(s) = space(s);

st(s) = stitch(es);

() = work directions in parentheses into same st;

[] = work directions in brackets the number of times specified;

* = repeat whatever follows the * as indicated.

Special Stitches

dtr (Double treble crochet) = [Yarn over] 3 times, insert hook in indicated stitch, yarn over and draw up a loop, [yarn over and draw through 2 loops on hook] 4 times.

sc2tog (Single crochet 2 together) = insert hook in next stitch, yarn over and draw up a loop, (2 loops on hook), insert hook in next stitch, yarn over and draw up a loop, yarn over and draw through all 3 loops on hook.

Special Technique

Adjustable-ring method—Wrap yarn in a ring, ensuring that the tail falls behind the working yarn. Grip ring and tail firmly between middle finger and thumb. Insert hook through center of ring, yarn over (with working yarn) and draw up a loop. Work stitches of first round in the ring. Pull gently, but firmly, on tail to tighten ring when instructed.

Notes

1. Blanket is made back and forth in rows, then border is worked in joined rounds.

2. Sixteen appliques of various sport balls are sewn to blanket. Details

on balls are added with embroidery.

3. Rattles are made in continuous rounds (spirals). Place marker for beginning of round and move marker up as each round is completed.

4. Before closing each rattle, insert a small ball with jingle bell inside (cat toy). As a safety precaution, place the cat toy in the toe of a knee high, tie securely, and trim off the excess hosiery. This will contain the pieces if the insert is crushed. Discard the rattle if the insert breaks.

5. Refer to sizes listed above for the appropriate hook for each section

6. To change color, work last stitch of old color to last yarn over. Yarn over with new color and draw through all loops on hook to complete stitch. Proceed with new color. Do not cut old color until instructed. Carry color not in use up side of piece until next needed.

7. Refer to photograph for placement of all embroidered details.

BLANKET

With largest hook and A, ch 69.

Row 1: Working in back bumps only, sc in 2nd ch from hook and in each ch across, turn - 68 sts.

Row 2: Ch 2 (does not count as a st here and throughout this section), hdc in each st across, turn.

43

Repeat Row 2 until blanket measures 25" (63.5 cm) long.

Border

Round 1 (right side): Ch 1, sc evenly across ends of rows of first side; working in opposite side of foundation ch, (sc, ch 1, sc) in first ch (corner made), sc in each ch to last ch, (sc, ch 1, sc) in last ch (corner made); sc evenly across ends of rows of other side; (sc, ch 1, sc) in first st (corner made), sc in each st to last st, (sc, ch 1, sc) in last st (corner made); join with slip st in first sc.

Round 2: Ch 2 (counts as first hdc here and throughout), hdc in each st around, working (2 hdc, ch 2, 2 hdc) in each corner ch-space; join with slip st in top of beginning ch.

Repeat Round 2 until blanket measures 35½" x 35½" (90 x 90 cm).

Next Round: Ch 1, sc in each st around, working (2 sc, ch 2, 2 sc) in each corner ch-2 space; join with slip st in first st.

Repeat last round, as needed, until blanket measures 36" x 36" (91.5 x 91.5 cm).

Fasten off.

Rattle Pocket

With largest hook and A, ch 26.

Row 1 (wrong side): Working in back bumps only, sc in 2nd ch from hook and in each ch across, turn - 25 sc.

Row 2: Ch 1, sc in first st, *ch 5, skip next 3 sts, sc in next st; repeat from * across, turn - 6 ch-5 spaces.

Row 3: Ch 7, sc in 3rd ch of first ch-5 space, *ch 5, sc in 3rd ch of next ch-5 space; repeat from * across, ch 2, dtr in last st (counts as ch 7), turn - 5 ch-5 sps and 2 ch-7 spaces.

Row 4: Ch 6, skip first ch-7 space, sc in 3rd ch of first ch-5 space, *ch 5, sc in 3rd ch of next ch-5 space; repeat from * across, ch 5, sc in 4th ch of beginning ch, turn - 6 ch-5 spaces.

Rows 5–16: Repeat Rows 3 and 4 six times.

Row 17: Ch 1, sc in first st, *3 sc in next ch-5 space, sc in next sc; repeat from * across, sc in last ch of beginning ch, turn - 25 sc.

Edging

Note When you are instructed to work in a stitch at the end of a row, the stitch may be a ch, sc, or dtr.

Round 1: Ch 1, 3 sc in first sc (corner made), sc in each sc across to last st, 3 sc in last sc (corner made); sc 31 sts evenly across ends of rows of side, working sc in each st and 3 sc in each ch-space; working on opposite side of foundation ch, 3 sc in first ch (corner made), sc in each ch across to last ch, 3 sc in last ch (corner made), sc 31 sts evenly across ends of rows of next side, working sc in each st and 3 sc in each ch-space; join with slip st in first sc - 120 sc (23 sc across top and bottom edge between 3-sc corners and 31 sc across sides between 3-sc corners).

Rounds 2 and 3: Ch 1, sc in each st around working 3 sc in center st of each 3-sc corner; join with slip st in first sc - 136 sc.

Fasten off, leaving a long tail for sewing.

Using photograph as a guide, position pocket to lower left corner of blanket, placing left side and bottom edge of pocket to edge of Round 1 of border. Sew in place on 3 sides leaving top edge open.

APPLIQUES

Football (make 4)

With hook appropriate to this section and B, ch 2.

Row 1 (right side): Work 2 sc in 2nd ch from hook, turn - 2 sc.

Row 2: Ch 1, 2 sc in each st across, turn - 4 sc.

Row 3: Ch 1, sc in first st, [2 sc in next st] twice, sc in last st, turn-6 sc.

Row 4: Ch 1, sc in first 2 sts, [2 sc in next st] twice, sc in last 2 sts, turn - 8 sc.

Row 5: Ch 1, sc in first 3 sts, [2 sc in next st] twice, sc in last 3 sts; change to C at end of row, turn - 10 sc. Drop, but do not cut, B.

Rows 6 and 7: Ch 1, sc in each st across, turn; change to B at end of Row 7. Cut C.

Rows 8 and 9: Ch 1, sc in each st across, turn.

Row 10: Ch 2 (counts as first hdc), sc in next 8 sts, hdc in last st, turn - 10 sts.

Rows 11–13: Ch 1, sc in each st across, turn.

Row 14: Repeat Row 10.

Row 15: Ch 1, sc in first 3 sts, [sc2tog] twice, sc in last 3 sts; change to C, turn - 8 sts. Drop, but do not cut, B.

Rows 16 and 17: Repeat Rows 6 and 7.

Row 18: Ch 1, sc in first 2 sts, [sc2tog] twice, sc in last 2 sts, turn-6 sts.

Row 19: Ch 1, sc in first st, [sc2tog] twice, sc in last st, turn - 4 sts.

Row 20: [Sc2tog] twice - 2 sts. Do not turn.

Edging

Round 1 (right side): Ch 1, with right side facing and working in ends of rows, sc evenly around; join with slip st in first st. Fasten off, leaving a long tail for sewing.

With C, embroider laces on football between Rows 7 and 16.

Basketball (make 4)

With hook size appropriate to this section and D, make an adjustable ring.

Round 1: Ch 1, 6 sc in ring; join with slip st in first st - 6 sc. Pull gently, but firmly, on tail to tighten ring.

Round 2: Ch 1, 2 sc in each st around; join with slip st in first st-12 sc.

Round 3: Ch 1, sc in first st, 2 sc in next st, *sc in next st, 2 sc in next st; repeat from * around; join with slip st in first st - 18 sc.

Round 4: Ch 1, sc in first 2 sts, 2 sc in next st, *sc in next 2 sts, 2 sc in next st; repeat from * around; join with slip st in first st - 24 sc.

Round 5: Ch 1, sc in first 3 sts, 2 sc in next st, *sc in next 3 sts, 2 sc in next st; repeat from * around; join with slip st in first st - 30 sc.

Round 6: Ch 1, sc in first 4 sts, 2 sc in next st, *sc in next 4 sts, 2 sc in next st; repeat from * around; join with slip st in first st - 36 sc.

Round 7: Ch 1, sc in first 5 sts, 2 sc in next st, *sc in next 5 sts, 2 sc in next st; repeat from * around; join with slip st in first st - 42 sc.

Fasten off, leaving a long tail for sewing.

With E, embroider 2 curved seam lines.

Baseball (make 4)

With hook size appropriate to this section and C, make an adjustable ring.

Rounds 1–5: Work same as Rounds 1–5 of basketball applique - 30 sc.
Fasten off, leaving a long tail for sewing.

With F, embroider 2 curved seam lines with hash marks.

Soccer Ball (make 4)

With hook size appropriate to this section and E, make an adjustable ring.

Rounds 1 and 2: Work same as Rounds 1 and 2 of basketball applique; change to C at end of Round 2 - 12 sc. Cut E.

Rounds 3–7: Work same as Rounds 3–7 of basketball - 42 sc.

Fasten off, leaving a long tail for sewing.

With E, embroider 6 hexagons around Round 2, stitching lower edge of each hexagon over 2 stitches of Round 2.

RATTLES

Football

With hook size appropriate to this section and B, ch 30; being careful not to twist ch, join with slip st in first ch.

Round 1: Working in back bumps, sc in each ch around- - 30 sc. Place marker for beginning of round and move marker up as each round is completed.

Rounds 2–4: Sc in each st around.

Round 5: *Sc in next 3 sts, sc2tog; repeat from * around; change to C at end of round - 24 sc. Drop, but do not cut B.

Rounds 6 and 7: Sc in each st around; change to B at end of Round 7. Cut C.

Round 8: *Sc in next 2 sts, sc2tog; repeat from * around - 18 sts.

Round 9: Sc in each st around.

Round 10: *Sc in next st, sc2tog; repeat from * around - 12 sts.

Round 11: *Sc2tog; repeat from * around – 6 sts. Fasten off, leaving a long tail for sewing.

Weave tail through last round and pull gently to close opening. Secure tail and weave in end.

Round 12: Working in opposite side of foundation ch, join B with slip st to first ch, ch 1, sc in each ch around - 30 sc. Place marker for beginning of round and move marker up as each round is completed.

Rounds 13 and 14: Sc in each st around.

Rounds 15–21: Repeat Rounds 5–11, inserting rattle mechanism and adding stuffing as you go before opening becomes too small.

Fasten off, leaving a long tail for sewing.

Weave tail through last round and pull gently to close opening. Secure tail and weave in end.

With 2 strands of C held together, embroider laces on football between Rounds 6 and 16.

Basketball

With hook appropriate to this section and D, make an adjustable ring.

Round 1: Ch 1, 6 sc in ring - 6 sc. Place marker for beginning of round and move marker up as each round is completed. Pull gently, but firmly on tail to tighten ring.

Round 2: Work 2 sc in each st around - 12 sc.

Round 3: *Sc in next st, 2 sc in next st; repeat from * around - 18 sc.

Round 4: *Sc in next 2 sts, 2 sc in next st; repeat from * around -24 sc.

Round 5: *Sc in next 3 sts, 2 sc in next st; repeat from * around -30 sc.

Round 6: *Sc in next 4 sts, 2 sc in next st; repeat from * around -36 sc.

Round 7: *Sc in next 5 sts, 2 sc in next st; repeat from * around -42 sc.

Rounds 8–17: Sc in each st around.

Round 18: *Sc in next 5 sts, sc2tog; repeat from * around - 36 sc.

Round 19: *Sc in next 4 sts, sc2tog; repeat from * around - 30 sc.

Round 20: *Sc in next 3 sts, sc2tog; repeat from * around - 24 sc. Insert rattle mechanism and add stuffing as you go before opening becomes too small.

Round 21: *Sc in next 2 sts, sc2tog; repeat from * around - 18 sc.

Round 22: *Sc in next st, sc2tog; repeat from * around - 12 sc.

Round 23: *Sc2tog; repeat from * around – 6 sc. Fasten off, leaving a long tail for sewing.

Add additional stuffing, if needed. Weave tail through last round and pull gently to close opening. Secure tail and weave in end.

Seam Line (make 3)

With smallest hook and E, work as many ch as necessary to fit seam line around basketball.

Using photograph as a guide, pin one seam line around circumference of ball and pin each remaining seam line midway between circumference and outer edge. With thread and sewing needle, sew seam lines to ball.

Baseball

With hook appropriate to this section and C, make an adjustable ring.

Rounds 1–5: Work same as Rounds 1–5 of basketball rattle - 30 sc.

Place marker for beginning of round and move marker up as each round is completed. Pull gently, but firmly, on tail to tighten ring.

Rounds 6–14: Sc in each st around.

Rounds 15–18: Repeat Rounds 20–23 of basketball rattle, inserting rattle mechanism in Round 16 and adding stuffing as you go - 6 sc.

Fasten off, leaving a long tail for sewing. Add additional stuffing, if needed. Weave tail through last round and pull gently to close opening. Secure tail and weave in end. With F, topstitch 2 sets of curved seam lines and hash marks around sides of ball.

FINISHING

Using photograph as a guide, pin appliques around border of blanket. With end tails, sew each applique to blanket.

Weave in ends.

Printed in Great Britain
by Amazon